The Dark Room Chronicles

A Collection of Poetry

The Dark Room Chronicles

A Collection of Poetry

Marnell Jones

authorHOUSE®

AuthorHouse™ LLC
1663 Liberty Drive
Bloomington, IN 47403
www.authorhouse.com
Phone: 1-800-839-8640

Published by AuthorHouse 12/02/2013

ISBN: 978-1-4918-3016-1 (sc)
ISBN: 978-1-4918-3017-8 (e)

Library of Congress Control Number: 2013919430

Any people depicted in stock imagery provided by Thinkstock are models, and such images are being used for illustrative purposes only. Certain stock imagery © Thinkstock.

This book is printed on acid-free paper.

Contents

Chapter Five

Introduction

The Dark Room Chronicles is an array of "Dark" poetry that was written during a very oppressive time in my life. It was very hard for me to see any light at the end of the tunnel on many of those days; and as you read, my poetry will reflect my state of mind. I hope that my poetry will give strength, encouragement, faith, and hope to those who can relate in any way to my poetry. Thank you to my family and friends for all your love and unwavering support.

Chapter One

Dark

Imagine a desolate existence, surrounded by a macabre of images, an ensemble of emotions has left his shadow forlorn

Trudging awkwardly up a jagged hill, his soul yearns for solace and to prevail against all odds

His spirit is full of pride, although his sad eyes tell a different tale, suffering beyond measure, insult added to injury, it's that transparent even visible enough to be heard

Followed faithfully by a hex that grabs and pulls at his taut neck with nails like razors, trying to drag him to his death but gods angels won't let it occur, so innocent so pure

With outstretched wings they float with halos, not speaking a word but their sheer presence lets him know . . . .

By Marnell Jones

A Thousand

It's hard to live with a thousand regrets, a thousand hurts that run deeper than the pacific ocean's depth, pain amplified a thousand times, makes it hard to breathe and even difficult to see straight

A thousand shattered dreams can easily be the equivalent, why are we born and why do we die? Is the question I've seemed to ask myself thousand times

In between life's mysterious cycle, I've had thousands smiles, a thousand frowns, a thousand up's, and a thousand down's

Every night before bed when I turn out the lights, over the years I've said a thousand prayers and shed a thousand tears underneath the moon's light

It seems as though a thousand of those prayers have been unanswered but I know that's blaspheme because god answers at the speed of light

A thousand of my wrongs that he made right, sad songs sung, a thousand, hidden fears a thousand, heartbreaks a thousand, a thousand . . . .

By Marnell Jones

Fictitious reality

Reality appears to be an illusion because when my raging flesh deteriorates and my tortured soul disintegrates and my weary spirit dissipates not one atom will be spared

When my physical merges with the essence and memory becomes my presence and my name is uttered only on occasion, just have an adamant amount of faith

It'll help you to survive, help you to rise and stay afloat like an unsinkable vessel, hope is what I plan to encounter, Ms. Serendipity prolific even has witnessed my tragedy

A somber tale of one's personal hell, of a sky so empty, not one star in sight and the once glowing moon has even lost It's light

Tomorrow's a new day and the future seems bright, despite my plight, god is good and I must continue life, my inevitable journey

By Marnell Jones

Surreal

When night falls and blankets the town, the moon and the stars are as bright as the gleam in the eye of a child

The aura is so majestic all living creatures become restless if not careful fall victim to heinous transgressions

The night is so surreal as I merge with my shadow, every creature of the night's call seem to echo, I feel complete solace at midnight with a warm breeze

My mind transforms into a kaleidoscope of vivid imagery, I transcend through the clouds, their as soft as cotton and the silence is so loud

Not seen but rather heard, a macabre of abstruse sound piercing through my soul, piercing through my guise, riding a wavelength of emotions I wearily sigh

The dark can be as lonely as the number one, as the moon begins to fade, giving rise to a beautiful morning sun

By Marnell Jones

Perdition

On my road to perdition it was clearly inevitable, leaving me in this crippling condition, yet this fascinating awkward journey in the midst of my existence, reality or the mind's eye perception, provides a kaleidoscope of vivid selections

Some extravagant, some ghastly but all speaks in high volumes of my atrocious prior actions, higher power please have mercy, I'm not perfect I'm earthly, my sunrise isn't perpetual, it's predestined to set

With a pendulum of anxiety in this stagnated society, does it matter however, if I'm unrighteously righteous or imperfectly perfect on this tragically sweet road to perdition.

By Marnell Jones

The journey

Nearing the end of the road, the journey has been quite arduous, For six lengthy years he's trudged in banal boots so solemnly, his feet are swollen and blistered but his spirit has been refined, for in order to reform one must go through the fire

The road was scattered with many oppressive obstacles to persevere through what may seem like the impossible to that man I pay homage, a true warrior, through combat he's battled many along the way and through each battle he victoriously emerged unscathed

Death before dishonor! He deserves a medal of valor, solitude, gloomy nights, locked in a lonesome cell, just me and my thoughts, a teardrop away from hell, so penitent and discontent flashing images of family and friends, in dire need of love, wants to be hugged, kissed, and touched

Instead isolation then it comes in icy whispers marching in military formation, demons, racing thoughts of death, fire and brimstone littered with torn pieces of flesh, panic attacks and I struggle to catch my breath, time passes as I endure this crippling condition and I soon regain order

Trials and tribulations, some physical though many were mental I survived! The gray clouds have dispersed to beautiful sunshine

By Marnell Jones

Regrets

I often wish that I could rewind time long enough to save my happiness, I would've rescued him from the pitfalls of perdition

I let that innocent, intelligent young boy die! I watched him take his last breath slowly, I didn't intervene nor try to resuscitate him, blame me!

Like a leaf blown in the wind or the gossamers of a dandelion, shattered dreams and mournful cries, he speaks from beyond, speaks in cold whispers that make my body shiver

He's cold alone and afraid in that isolated place, I didn't love him enough now he's gone, my only boy, the missing piece to my aching heart like a blemished piece of art, my spirit is forever tarnished so unfathomable but the picture is all too real, it's vivid, it has feelings and emotions, it hurts, it bleeds, it dies but still needs me, he needs me, we need me, I need me!

By Marnell Jones

Alone

Imagine living an isolated existence with silence so persistent it blocks all five senses becoming louder than your thoughts, so I fervently pray to my god on this dark dismal day and still against my shackled will, sunshine becomes bland to the blind eyes of the saintly old woman with unsteady, trembling hands

Eight decades of experience, a macabre of imagery may have shattered overtime her once innocent vision, how easily dreams can be diminished, slipping through your fingers like sand or evaporating like dew after a misty night's rain never to be replenished without hope once again

Emotional adversity this pain is unfathomable, I spoke with this entity, quite friendly who gave me this black rose then kissed me so softly that my gloomy aura began to glow, how tragically sweet to hear what's not being said, vibes are the senses spider web, wrapped in a blanket of hurt, firmly so hot and unsafe he manages although his tormented spirit has gotten use to this dreadful place

By Marnell Jones

Entice

Your eyes are like enticing waving pools of purple fire, I'm hypnotized and so grateful to swim in your desire, the windows to your angelic soul possess a depth of knowledge that some men may never know, you turn me on with your intellect, brains and beauty, sultry dialect, labia moist and loins erect, you're everything and more

A woman, my sexy vixen, perfect nymph teases me with sweet warm kisses, keeping me perpetually aroused, with fire engine colored lipstick, you're so hot baby, I create sun spots on your neck as I gingerly bite, you sensually moan and you love how I skillfully seduce, it's hard to control myself when I'm deep inside of you

My animal instinct surges for your honey flavored womanhood my drenched face emerges, you're puzzling, yet dazzling, mysteriously, teasing a challenge keeps me balanced my dangerous addiction, stimulating conversation, French kissing oral lectures your velvet tongue with lips so soft it really drives me crazy, this sensation is so surreal but keeps me so elated

Body language down to earth but speaks in high volumes, eye contact is so erotic I sense what you think in between each and every suspended blink, so naughty and exotic

By Marnell Jones

Torture

Why do I torture myself? Is it because I love living close to the edge, I love playing with fire, feeling it burn getting so close to death

I think there's something wrong with my head I'm directing this movie and my actions have become my plot

My goal is to survive, I look at life as a test and all I can do is give it my best, go hard or go home is the motto, I try to lead and not follow, I try to give and not borrow, and be happy with less sorrow

There's a better tomorrow but I fear it may never come there's a war inside of me and the battle is far from won, I cry internally because externally the tears won't shed

I really want to cry and not play tough all the time but the world is such a lonely place, ice cold stares and morbid attitudes how did living get to this magnitude?

Highly misunderstood but god is all too good, a wrong turn at the fork road I now realize but many will never have a clue

By Marnell Jones

Chapter Two

Mother

O'mother o'mother like you there's no other, amidst a violent storm you always provide cover and despite your lifestyle you've always shown unconditional love

To me you're the best mother sent directly from the lord above, the bible says honor thy mother and thy father and I do

Without you there's no me and without me there's no you, you'd take your last breath for me sacrifice your own life for me, you're there for me morally and complete every part of me

You, my sister and granny, I thank god that I have such a family, I have such beautiful childhood memories and close to my heart I hold each one dearly

Mother's day should be celebrated everyday because you're the best and I love you

By Marnell Jones

Love

A closer look at a broken heart a new found love for a new start, tongue kissing is a French art

I like your body but I love that you're smart, you make love to my mind which send shivers down my spine

I think of you often and sometimes I feel lost when you're not around, I can't sleep, can't eat and can hardly breathe

I gasp for your touch, for your kiss, for your love my vixen sent to me directly from the lord, you're the other half of me, anything you need just ask of me and the only thing I ask of you is to give me a child, take part in my fantasies and take that walk down the aisle

By Marnell Jones

Bond

The bond that we have and the love we both share remains to grow stronger each blessed year

I often wish that I had two lives just to spend each of them with you, so that means I'd marry you twice and we'd have two kids

We'd make love over two million times and love each other twice as much even to the end

My soul mate, my lover, my friend, do you believe in love at first sight or what about fate? well, when I first laid eyes on you I knew right then that you'd always be in my life, I cherish your thoughts and you're sassy attitude keeps me in line, you radiate this alluring aura and your body is so fine

My personal Nefertiti, black queen I need you, without you there's no me and the sky would collapse and the air I would not be able to breathe

With each beat of my heart, a vision of your pretty face pops into my mind, I can't wait to suck those honey sweet lips and you definitely have the most beautiful smile

By Marnell Jones

Fantasy

If I could just hold your soft hands, while staring in your mesmerizing eyes, as beautiful as a warm, clear summer night, the stars are like pinkish-blue diamonds with a full moon shining bright

You get me so high, the lady of my dreams, the love of my life, my wife, my everything, your beautiful skin is like fireworks bursting in the sky, your attitude, your mind, your thoughts are like fine red wine

I often thank god for giving me the opportunity to be a part of your future, which is now my present, loving you, to perpetually be in love with you, like a spiraling river of love, our emotions are intertwined and I hope you know that I'll always be there for you down to the last second of the end of time

You're have my heart in your prison and you're constantly on my mind I can't shake this addiction I must have you all the time, you're so passionately passionate, each night I must ravish you I thirst for you, greatly and your love juice keeps me satisfied, the mother of my unborn seeds conceived through the mind

By Marnell Jones

A gangster's death

There's nothing like dying tragically on a hot summer day, with a bright blue sky and the birds even chirp while you're facing death

It was quiet before the storm and I didn't notice the burning at first, chaos and hateful glares spread across my killer's face

I commend them on their kill, for I've killed many men in my day

But only now do I realize my victims suffering and pain but nonetheless I'm a G and pride forces me to shoot back

I hit up the front and rear passenger side doors and blew out their back windows, they must've had big guns because I had in and out wounds through my stomach and out my back

A slug in my leg and two more in my chest, my lungs collapse and so do I, I piss myself as I try to catch my breath

Damn! Look at all these women and little kids screaming and crying telling me not to die, if only I could respond back telling them I'll try

The intense pain won't allow me to speak and my mother's crying kissing my cheek; it's funny because my thoughts are crystal clear, I'm aware, I can hear but my body's getting cold, very cold and I know death is near

All the sins that I've committed and especially the four men that I've killed, flash before my eyes and my heart's beating becomes still

By Marnell Jones

Frozen tears

I've been trying to cry but the tears just won't fall, my eyes are as dry as the sand under the burning Sahara sun

It's not that my heart is made of ice, nor, is my soul I truly seem to suffer from stunted emotional growth

I'm full of empathy and compassion but I always hurt and maim, when I'm alone at night just me and the dark, I often reflect on my actions and my conscience comes into play

I think therefore I am, so all of my past experiences and memories make me who I am but who will I be tomorrow if a part of me dies today?

Why does wrong seem so right? considered an outlaw of society, I'm your every sinister thought in the flesh, every transgression you've ever committed I'm it!

I'm alive walking dead slowly burning in hell, so when you stare In my eyes it speaks volumes of my tale, a tale of pain and hurt, a bleak future hope is obsolete, I'm a statistic predestined to be what I am and where I reside since my unplanned birth in 1983

By Marnell Jones

The chase

Peace, a feeling of serenity an abstract thought even in a world full of atrocities, transgression, and negativity

Solace is futile, not one lake is placid, perpetual chaos continues action, no rest or relaxation, no peace in sight

Peace of mind I yearn for, even in my slumber there's war, casualties of catastrophe, emotionally scarred, so painfully stark, transparent in the dark

Nowhere to hide, I'm weary and my eyes have begun tearing as I shutter from the cold, in my heart there's a hole with shackles around my soul

I only want peace, I often pray to my god loudly and passionately amongst sorrowful sobs, why do you run from me constantly? I can't keep up with your pace, you're quick easily transcending time and space, over large bodies of water and even continents I'll continue the chase

By Marnell Jones

Ebony love

Baby you're so gorgeous from your head to your toes, you delight each of my five senses and your ebony skin glows

Your beautiful hair is like a thousand midnights and I often fantasize of my lips touching yours and I can even taste the licorice on your plush velvet tongue

Oh, how I would sale my soul just to inhale your sweet scent, the scent of your favorite perfume dabbed gently on the sides of your neck, down to your scrumptious honey fragrance between those thick thighs

I would love to caress your breasts and roll my probing tongue over your sweet hard nipples and suck on your flesh, until your gasping for breath

I could swim in your soul as I stare in those dark mysterious eyes, I sense heartbreak, slightly bewildered because I just can't figure out why, any man would hurt you, instead of thanking god that he has you by his side

You're a goddess, a queen, the lady of my dreams . . . . My waking thought, my sunshine and the air that I breathe

By Marnell Jones

Autumn

The wind blows and leaves rustle, a silent scene, alone and as lonely as one can be

Silent screams and exaggerated expressionless faces, the crushing pain of a hurtful heartbreaking

Why? I ask on many occasions, gray is the mood, a real dull like gray as gray as the clouds on a stormy day

To calm my fears and send evil away I pray, I stand and I pray, I sit and I pray, I lay and I pray each night I pray

It helps, I heal just enough to face another day, get tortured, shed tears, pray then recuperate

A cycle as common as life and death and far more addictive then drugs or sex, it's beautiful to the point it gets ugly then separates

As then as the line between love and hate but as beautiful as the act of loving making

By Marnell Jones

Passion

Passionately French kissed, true pure bliss and stagnated thoughts, caressed in between warm snickers your hour glass figure drives me mad

When you kiss me ever so softly blood oozes to the lower part of my anatomy, I can't describe this feeling, no words within the human vocabulary

I lust for you hysterically, your body's so velvety and warm, reminding me of kneaded dough as I run my fingers up and down your smooth torso

Your pudgy stomach jiggles when I blow it and you love each and every moment, I adore everything about you, everything you dislike when you stare in the mirror, I love

You deserve a ring, you're my queen and your bath water I'll surely drink, I'll die for you, ill cry with you, the mother of my unborn seed

I'm your man, protector and provider, you're my girl, supporter and nurturer, baby let's grow old together

By Marnell Jones

Chapter Three

Will Power

My life hasn't exactly turned out the way I expected, I'm strong so I cope with life's rollercoaster kismet

It's just another test that the lord has given me and I refuse to let this test turn into a total fiasco, I'll beat it just like the rest and dance under the bright moon's light

My imperturbable demeanor, mixed with the strong will of a winner, no one or no situation can force me to live in a state of hysteria

I bask in my family's love daily that I wear as my amulet, fear does not live in my heart but god does and with his spirit in me all is conquerable

This imbroglio is so minute compared to other people's trouble and I'm very blessed to even say that, I now face life with complete ebullience; me and the universe are in complete unity

Everything and everyone seems to be even more beautiful, I'm a survivor and survive is what I will always do

By Marnell Jones

Summer Blush

Golden colored dandelions and pretty flickering butterflies, the grass is so green against bright blue skies

The sun reflects off of your shining eyes as you stare back in mine, your eyes are like a full moon on a warm summer night and I always seem to lose my train of thought when you glare at me just right

You truly nurture my soul and complete me as a man, my beautiful sweet nymph's soft velvet lips, fills my spirit lift with each and every kiss

Ebony Isis all I need is you on a deserted island, I'd quench my thirst with love juice from your labia, every meal would be desert as I glide my salivating tongue over your luscious womanly curves

You're truly everything a woman should be and more and without you in my life, my world would be empty for sure

By Marnell Jones

Spirit Bones

Holocaust of lost black souls, expressionless faces of the spirit bones

From deep below their watery graves, they cry out for me I am their pain Asphyxiate, I try to breathe but the weight of shame pulls me deep

Sadistic atrocities mix with the stench of fear, macabre images the end is near, So I pray and gasp for breath to not be the next spirit bone but I am the last one left

By Marnell Jones

Bleeding Heart

This bleeding heart encased within a steel vault

With no combination or key, no button for self-release just

Self-pity and even that doesn't work

A kaleidoscope of hurts, unsure of my own shadow, love-less lurks

It haunts and taunts perpetually looming like one's conscience

A conscience full of transgressions, regrets and unlearned lessons

Raised to be better not the latter, between me, myself and I and they we chatter

Of the past often before purity was lost in, what is now and even then

Considered Babylon, nostalgia reigns hot and humid like a summer night's rain, The lonely heart that plays a somber tune, on his golden saxophone to past visions of his matriarch and siblings, His beloved matriarch now resting in eternal sleep, Effect perpetual heartache to siblings are like sand in ones hands, their slipping away, dust to a fan

Time doesn't wait it disobeys, a permanent qualm

I ponder the effects of my actions, life seemed so simpler back then, the sun shined differently, it beamed happily, brightly like an infant's smile, His soul yearns for yester-years, weary of pain, a river of tears, maximum losses and minimum gains, To question ones' mortality against an unnatural imbalance, before final answer he wishes for that bond, tight like a firm handshake, a bond that love creates, a bond that doesn't separate . . . EVER

A monster's insecurities

Being vulnerable I care too much

And I hate it! I'm so misunderstood and emotional, I'm

Too complex for those who have no patience For if you lack

Understanding my pain can be overbearing but I try my best to understand you I guess empathy is in my nature but I'm the

Sinner and you're the saint, with two different colors of the same

Portrait we paint

A scarlet letter upon my forehead I love hard so

Stay away from me I beg, I live in contradiction, I really want you

To get close to becoming familiar with every fiber of my being and

Not to disappear on me like a ghost, Am I too sensitive or do I

Come off as insecure? I'm a melting pot of these feelings and it's boiling within my soul

I often feel unsure abundant estrogen who knows

Or maybe I'm too mental, I over analyze and it shows, I didn't

Mean to build a wall I just wanted to cross the bridge to your heart

Now this distance I feel between us is totally my fault, or is it that

I talk too much and express myself to a fault, or whatever the problem

I wish that it were not, I toss and turn in my sleep, I lack desire to eat but I only want to know one thing, is it you or is it me??

Fork In The Road

I think and dream quite often I ponder, without one blink from a soul so somber

Without a word spoken, whispered or uttered, emotion so deep, he shivers and shutters Passionate, charismatic and yet lives so tragic.

Ugly and evil with a life so traumatic, for pain and death paradise he won't enter, at that fork in the road his spirit now stands splintered

Sin was his mentor but he now begs for forgiveness, In the midst of time and space the present stands still and his past is erased

Only time will tell if his future will take place

By Marnell Jones

No Pity

To sob for a lost soul and wallow in a pool full of

Salty tears, dread is gaining momentum with a belly full of
fear

The taste is quite acrid, metallic even and the smell leaves
him nauseous

Entity don't pity me, slay with no mercy, for if roles were
reversed

I'd murder you quite hurriedly

The spirit like glass broken has been shattered, heart
hollowed and

His veins have bled dry and that radiant light that once use
to glimmer has begun to dim in his vacant eyes

By Marnell Jones

Fervently

If my belief may fail amongst ghouls and

Perverted shadows and sunset prevails, light guide the way,

I was led astray

I beg for forgiveness, fervently, I've practiced redemption to make amends to those who I've maimed To that soul I slaughtered

Whose death is my perpetual pain, the earth cries its acidic rain,

Bombarded by human transgressions, its soil permeated with the stench of life's lessons, We are the same I look to the sky and rise

Celestial being, There's no concept of time, just the idea of being

One and unestranged from the mind

By Marnell Jones

If Only

If I could only hold your soft hands while kissing your succulent lips

To inhale your sweet strawberry scent, while staring in your

Mesmerizing eyes, as beautiful as a clear warm summer night

The stars are like pinkish-blue diamonds with a full moon shining bright, you get me so high, the lady of my dreams, and the love of my life, my wife, my everything

Your smooth skin tone in my eyes is like fireworks bursting In the sky;

Your attitude, your mind, your thoughts are like fine red wine, I often thank god for creating your parents, for creating you which has allowed me the opportunity of loving you; in the future which is now my present to perpetually be in love with you

Like a spiraling river of love, our emotions are intertwined and I hope you know that I'll always be there for you, down to the last second of time; you have my heart in your prison and you're constantly on my mind

I can't shake this addiction I crave you all the time, you're so passionately passionate, each night I must ravish you, I thirst for you greatly and your love juice keeps me satisfied, the mother of my unborn seed conceived from the mind

By Marnell Jones

Chapter Four

Emotional Logic

The mind meets heart and logic greets emotion

As intricate conversations start

A ballet of confused reasoning, the mind always whispers but the heart refuses to listen

Because of emotion logic is tossed out of the window, now forced to deal with a voluminous emotion, namely love

Love is good but love often hurts and the mental is brung back into the picture

Logic says she can't love you because her love belongs to him but emotion says she loves me too and thinks of me more, if not more than him

Irrational maybe, illogical yes but emotion and logic are two systems that will never mesh

By Marnell Jones

Relentless Love

My love for you is infinite and with you the impossible

Becomes possible

I appreciate you, I applaud you, I worship the ground you walk on

When I'm with you the sun shine's brighter, the air is fresher and

My heart beats lighter, without you my soul is castaway, I'll perish

I'll surely die, the birds will stop singing and the earth will begin to cry

You're my life, my thoughts, so ubiquitious indeed

You're my all in totality and my completion to everything

By Marnell Jones

Mockery

Fitful sleep and macabre dreams

This tortured soul in silence screams

Amongst the people in shame he suffers

Some gawk and snarl as his heavy heart flutters

A Mockery! His spirit weary, he heavily sighs

And his eyes become teary but deep within anger

Begins to rise and passion sails

With fortitude his strength prevails, their eyes watch

Wide with fear, of what he can become and is destined to

Be . . . . great!

By Marnell Jones

Ms. Brown

Brown sugar as sweet as lemon ice tea, mixed with four sugar cubes, my sweet tooth she satisfies me

Motivational conversation, she's almost too nice and every wise word of wisdom rolls off her tongue with the sweet scent of cherry pie

Every day that I inhale her sweet scent which often smells of pomegranates and licorice, just to be near her electrifies my smell and sight sense

With eyes like heaven and skin like honey, just to know her makes me so lucky

By Marnell Jones

A Man

I strive to be a better man, a man of vision, a man with a plan

A man of god, a one woman's man, a man amongst men, as well as a family man

An ocean of emotions I drown amongst the waves, the tide is high and the moon is full but will my life be saved

A man with flailing arms I inhale and exhale, a breath away from an early grave

So this man closes his eyes, holds his breath and begins to pray

By Marnell Jones

Sojourn His Truth

This weary soul tired and drained, emotionally, mentally and physically pained

Demon after demon his battered soul left clinging to a life that once was

A decade without love, a decade without a kiss, a decade without touch, a hardened heart is like damaged art, truly such a tragedy, even beating vanity

By Marnell Jones

Infatuation

Nonstop thoughts of her, infatuation of a love demure

Reign supreme, lodged within my heart, the lovely sound of her voice is able to arouse

Chocolate skin, soft thick ebony lips how I emphatically want to kiss, if done only in the dark I can surely keep a secret

Her demeanor, her style of grace, her pineapple perfume, her honey it makes me want to taste

Her inner beauty rivals the outer, the way she thinks and her depth of character

I've never met a woman like her; she's really one of a kind, special a rare gem, a pretty flower from leaf to stem

By Marnell Jones

Insanity

I've done the same things over and over again expecting different results, pure insanity, chances of winning are none to svelt

Got to quit while ahead, live life and not live dead, have to make my mother proud my grandmothers' in the sky smile

There's no future in prison, no future in frontin', just emotional growth stunted

Cell bars, white walls and prison yards is so detrimental to the mind you get so use to the dark that you squint when the sun shines

This is not me, I must prosper, two steps forward without one falter and two more prayers for the one last night forgotten

By Marnell Jones

Happy Day

My days are as bright as the stars are at night, my soul is full and my spirit's in flight

There's no hurt, just joyful tears, no pain no worries, no hidden fears

Carefree is my attitude, happiness is my destiny, I refuse to let myself get the best of me

No god, no peace, know god, know peace, the sooner you realize that, the better off you'll be

A loud thought in a quiet room, a whisper louder than a sonic boom

An invisible vision connected to an intense sensation but as beautiful as the arrow formed from geese migration

It's him, believe and have faith

By Marnell Jones

Chapter Five

Survive

There's so much living to do so I live, so I dream, so I hope that I do, survive

To have enough memories stored in my brain for two lifetimes, a

Kaleidoscope of images, soothing pleasant visions, waterfalls sounds and

The angels that created them

The sky blue heavens with its puffy white clouds, hanging low over

Kenya hear the hungry lion growl, the trees are so tall, leaves green, birds fly, the ant is small, try to envision this image if you were now just a child

The world is big, my thoughts are loud, my heart is passion and my lips are a smile, walk with me, lets' throw caution to the wind

By Marnell Jones

Ageless

A blind man whose deaf and can't speak, cannot chew food without his

False teeth He's in his golden years with a mind full of joyful memories, his

Skin is wrinkled and his hair gray, he misses the days of his youth but would never trade his current age

75 with a healthy heart, still cigarette smoking and every now and then a phlegm filled cough interrupt his breathing

Wife beater stained from greasy pork bacon, originally from Georgia

Before the big move to Newark, a down home boy, so pork he'll always

Love

His wife has been dead some twenty odd years, he often weeps for her through silent tears

The world is cold and he's blind but he prays and reads the bible in braille and if only this man could talk I'm quite sure he'd have many stories to tell

By Marnell Jones

Strong sister unique

Strong sister unique profound in her ways, her actions speak louder than words each day

Hard worker god made to endure, her supernatural strength surpasses that of man, she was born not to say I can't but rather I can! Strong sister unique loves her family and cures sickness with hands that heal, how very unselfish, bless her soul

Her smile has a luminous glow and when the blind hear her speak their minds' envision wings and a golden halo

Trial and tribulation equal 50% of her ambition and the other 50% is natural intuition, never settle for less, achieve and rise, those words speak in volumes in her determined eyes

Harriet Tubman, Angela Davis and Assata Shakur are all strong sisters' unique, Shiquonne, Torriah, and Lavissa Cromwell are now added to that list

Guided by the finest wisdom of this earth, our grandmother Ms. Mattie Tillman

These women have significantly changed the lives, mind and souls of the many they've encountered, without a strong sister unique, there's no doubt about it that your life will be incomplete

By Marnell Jones

Role Reversal

They say the old is really young and the young is really old

Roles are reversed and time waits for no man

Who are you? And who do you choose to be?

Is it in yours mind or is it reality? Is my reality yours or mine

Please somebody tell me I ask questions that appear to have no answers

Wake up from this conscious slumber the power of the mind is a universal wonder, I wonder idly, obviously blind, as blind as the man who doesn't see the woods for the trees

Why is there dark in my light? Is it the same reason that turns day into night? I'm scared, so scared I can feel it in my bones

I know I really do, I can feel it in my soul, who pays attention to the beating of their heart? If so it's a curse to finish before you start

The gleam of an eye, the salty taste of tears, the anxiety of facing your fear, never physical, all mental, I'm tired but I refused to lay, instead I opt to struggle another day

By Marnell Jones

Tug Of War

The faraway look in a man's eyes, The distance between space and time, the link between the soul and the mind, thoughts are like the gravitationl pull between the moon and tides, caught between a rock and a hard place, a sandstorm in a dry place, so how does one survive? How does one beat the odds? The difference between life and death is a breath away from god

I hope that my good deeds outweigh my transgressions, another breath a away from demise, a snip away from close family ties, the pain to fight back a tear, the strength to let it run then dry

The courage to face my fear, to stay strong and not run and hide, sometimes I have too much of it, sometimes it falls by the waste side

Some would call it pride, because of it many men have died; women have suffered due to false pride

Children don't know the difference, so in between it they sit and cry, my innocence has since vanished, vashished like passed time, now my disappointments reign supreme and my dreams reflect my state of mind

By Marnell Jones

The Entity

The past haunts him, traps him and won't let him go, street poisoned and it can't let him go, Hasn't paid for his sins yet and those demons still lurk, partially damaged mind, body, and soul

So young yet so old, something awaits in the trenches calling his name and he dreads each visit

Was he that horrible? He thinks but does not know, surely being tortured in this life for a past life, emotional rollercoaster

How much can he take? Just wants to be in a solid state of mind but something is terribly wrong

He cries and prays and reaches to the sky for hope but there's nothing but dark, cold loneliness with an ending before the start

By Marnell Jones

Lost Cause

I often wonder like an idle thought lost in outer space

Traveling from one destination to the next, just to arrive at the same place, surrounded by many strange faces

Feeling awkward, I slowly move forward pass each blurry figure with bright emerald and crimson colored eyes

My body feels heavy and each step is highly exaggerated, I wonder will I make it and with that thought I vanish

I'm one with the particles that form the high heavens, I float on the wind and in between breezes I dash in and out

I am of no form just an epiphany waiting to happen, a moment in time waiting to be captured, that electrical impulse from thought that creates action

The force of life, universal light that illuminates the darkest of nights

By Marnell Jones

Time Lapse

All alone in a lonely place, a silent breeze with many strange faces

He moves at a slow pace but everything seems to be a blur

The world is spinning; the beginning is the ending, he acts without thinking and wishes for hope

Prays for better days silently with no words spoken, with eyes closed and teeth clenched, circulation cut off from a balled up fist

How did his life come to be? He searches for answers, up—high and down—low

Converses with lost spirits who swim in his fiery soul, his once bright future is now bleak, his strong frame becomes weak, seconds turn to minutes and days become weeks

By Marnell Jones

G-Spot

Sweet lady take my hands, look in my eyes and tell me I'm your man

Kiss my lips, than suck my tongue, your love is like air that I need in my lungs

You keep me alive; you keep me sane, without you in my life, I'd feel a great deal of pain

Your soft hands and gentle touch, your intellect and personality keep me stuck

You amaze and keep me dazzled, now please baby hold me, I squeeze you tight and have you trapped in a seductive love trance

Suspended in time, sweat rolls down your cleavage, I wipe, then lick, you moan and then mumble, yeah baby that's it!

I give you what you want, ask for, or need; I'll do anything you desire because you're my queen

By Marnell Jones